The Ghostly Tales of St. Charles

Published by Arcadia Children's Books
A Division of Arcadia Publishing, Inc.
Charleston, SC
www.arcadiapublishing.com

First published 2025
Manufactured in the United States

Designed by Jessica Nevins
Images used courtesy of Shutterstock.com; p. 2 Ryanzo W. Perez/Shutterstock.com; p. 6 RN Photo Midwest/Shutterstock.com; p. 22 Smallbones/File:Newbill-McElhiney House.JPG/Wikimedia Commons; p. 40 briantium/Shutterstock.com; p. 54 briantium/Shutterstock.com; p. 74 Ryanzo W. Perez/Shutterstock.com; p. 80 Smallbones/File:1st Capitol St Charles MO.JPG/Wikimedia Commons; p. 102 10 Cows Photos/Shutterstock.com.

ISBN: 9781467196048
Library of Congress Control Number: 2025936379

Spooky America

THE GHOSTLY TALES OF ST. CHARLES

NICKI JACOBSMEYER

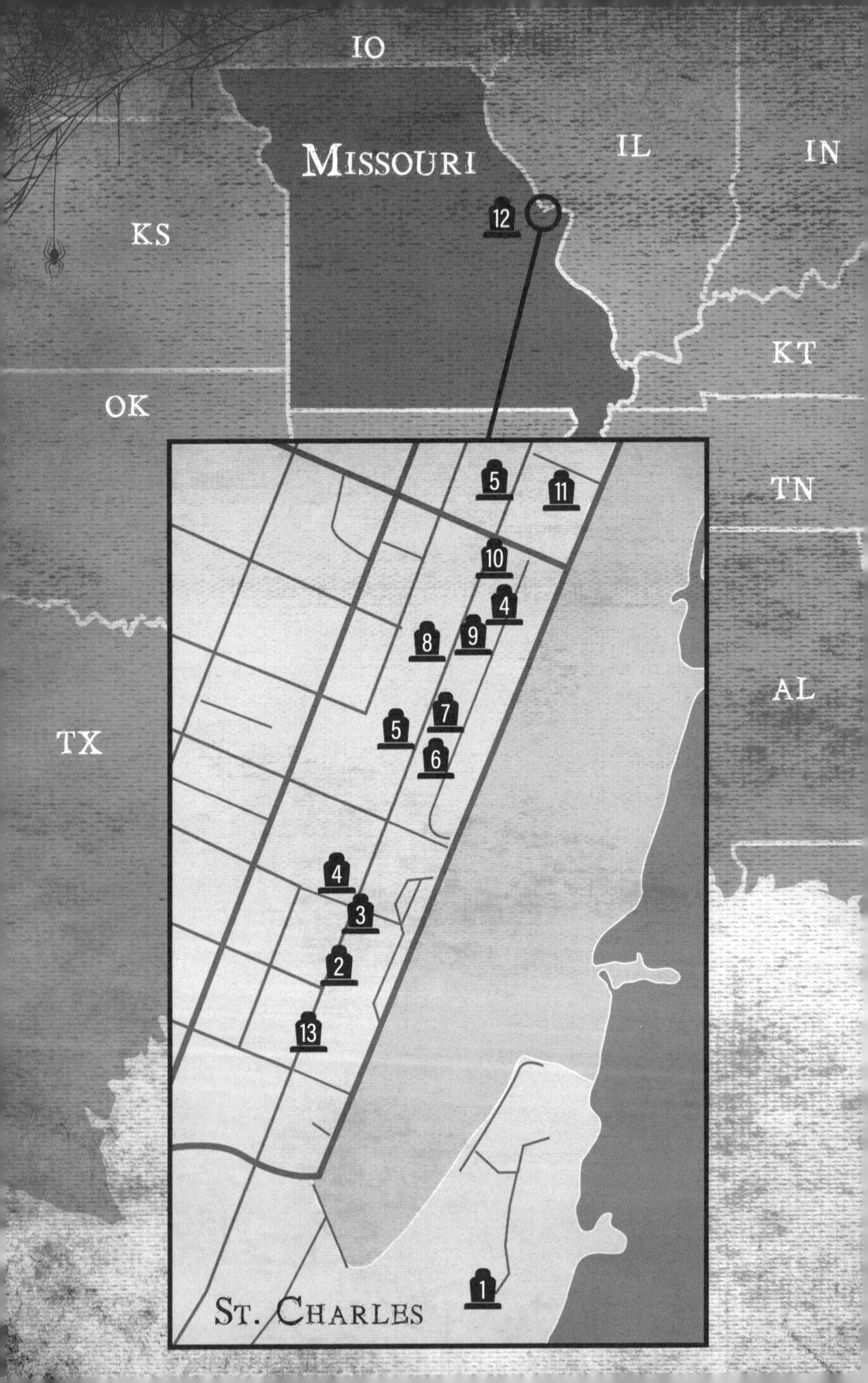

IO
Missouri
IL
IN
KS
12
KT
OK
5
11
TN
10
4
8
9
AL
7
5
TX
6
4
3
2
13
1
St. Charles

Table of Contents & Map Key

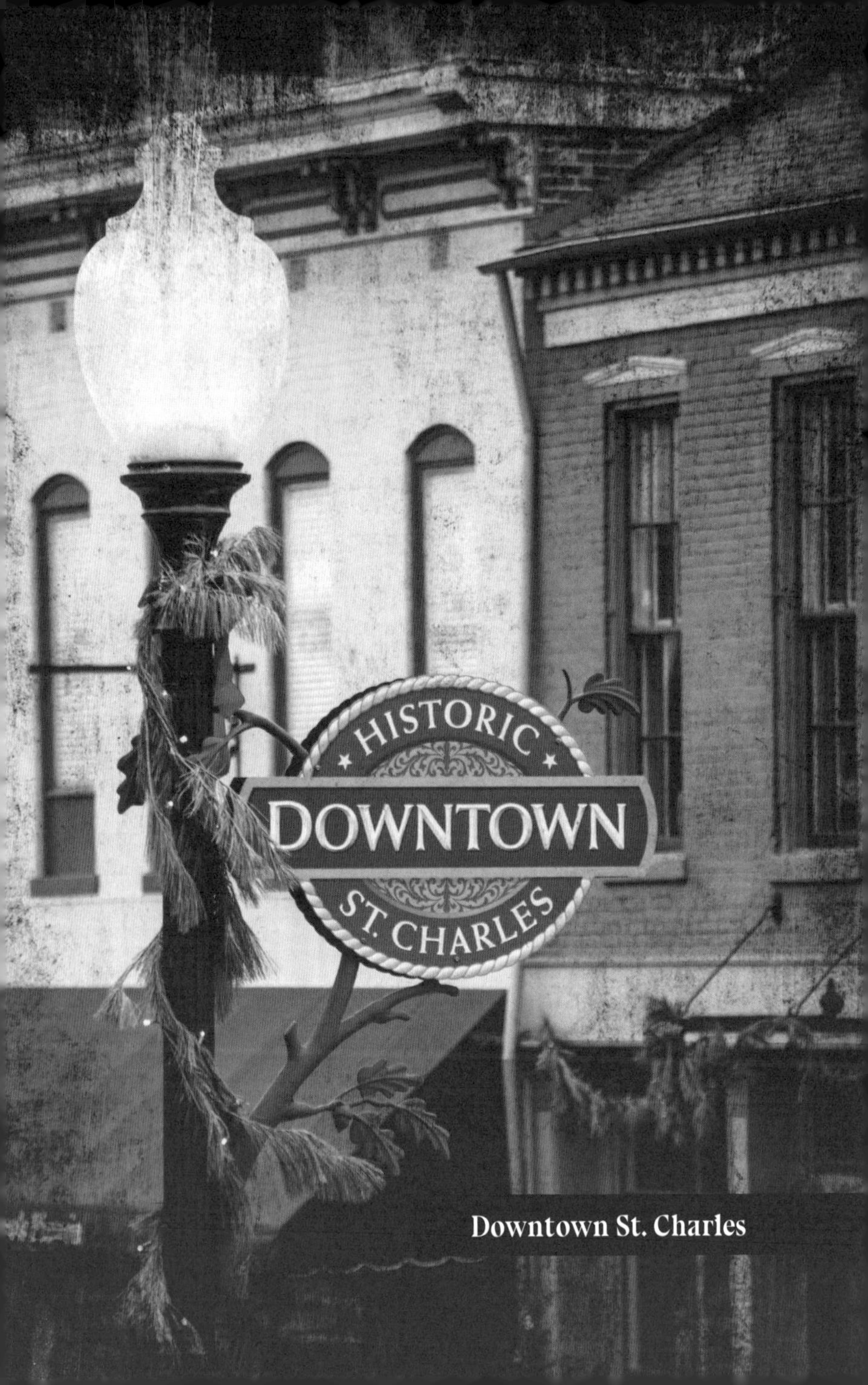

Downtown St. Charles

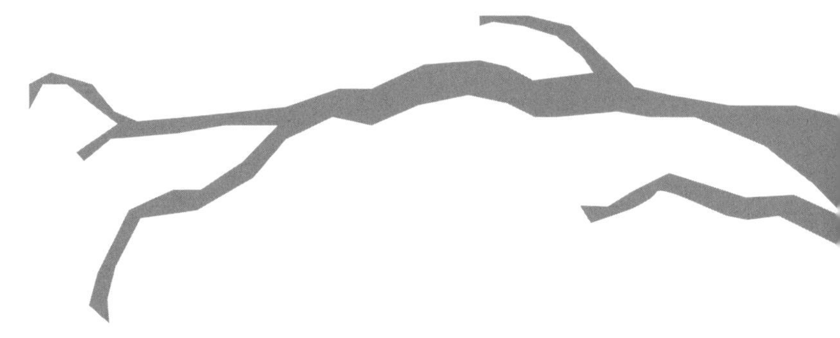

Welcome to Spooky St. Charles!

Care to join me on a stroll down a brick-paved street, aglow with gaslight, through a charming Missouri town that once welcomed pioneers and explorers?

You might even catch a glimpse of these historic figures peering around a corner. Perhaps you'll hear their footsteps traipsing down the staircase in one of the buildings. Still up for a stroll? Like you, the visitors over the past two hundred years are in no hurry to leave St. Charles. Whether it's your active imagination or something more, only you can decide.

St. Charles was once called Les Petites Côtes, "The Little Hills," when it was founded in 1769 by French Canadian fur trader Louis Blanchette. Between 1762 and 1800, the Spanish government controlled the Mississippi Valley and "The Little Hills" became "San Carlos Borromeo." In 1804, the famous explorers Lewis and Clark met here on the banks of the mighty Missouri River to begin their westward expedition. Shortly after, the city became known as "Saint Charles."

During the nineteeth century, German settlers brought their food, fellowship, and commerce to this thriving pioneer town. In the twentieth century, residents worked to preserve homes and stores throughout the area. Main Street St. Charles is the home of a Nationally Registered Historic District where you can eat, shop, and stay in the same buildings as these early explorers.

More history can be found at the St. Charles County Historical Society at 101 South Main Street. The city's two-story brick building used to be the Market House where meat and produce were sold. City offices were on the second floor. From 1886 to 1979, the building served as the St. Charles City Hall until it became the St. Charles County Historical Society in 1982. Although experts on local history can be found at the historical society, you're on your own when it comes to ghosts.

With almost one million visitors each year, not including the residents of the past, it makes you wonder how many spooky stories are out there. Come along—if you dare—and discover some of the tales of spooky St. Charles!

Lewis & Clark Boat House and Museum

Mysterious Museum

Down on the banks of the Missouri River, the Lewis & Clark Boat House and Museum is dying (shall we say) for visitors. Opened in the summer of 2003, the two-story building transports you to the nineteenth century from the moment you arrive. Here, you can relive Lewis & Clark's remarkable 1804–1806 expedition and explore the very place where they made their final preparations before heading into the unknown American wilderness.

Although it's been over two hundred years

since Lewis and Clark and their company of men headed upstream on the Missouri River in the keelboat, their journals remain. And as some St. Charles residents believe, the pages of text and maps may not be the *only* thing left behind . . .

One evening, the museum director and his son decided to have their own adventure and spend the night at the museum. Choosing to sleep on the second-floor, they spread out their sleeping bags. Since an indoor pond took up the middle of the vaulted room, they slept on either side. Before turning in for the night, they watched videos on their phones to help them relax. Instead of getting sleepy, however, they became aware of murmuring. They paused their videos to make sure they weren't just hearing background noise. But the sound didn't stop. Instead, the murmurs continued and even grew stronger, as if they were next door to a crowded party. How could this be? Father and son were the only two souls in the museum. Or were they?

On a separate occasion, the director's

family visited the museum after hours. His four-year-old granddaughter sauntered down the hallway, excited to explore. Since they had the place to themselves, they weren't worried about her getting lost.

The little girl stumbled upon a heavy door that linked a museum hallway to the restrooms. Normally, the door was closed and rarely used by visitors or staff. So, it was odd when the girl became captivated.

She called out for her grandpa.

Curious, he met her in the hallway.

His granddaughter pointed at the door and said, "Where did the man go?"

Confused, since the museum was closed, he asked her to explain. The little girl said that she'd seen a man march through the door and that she'd wanted to follow him. Was it just a child's vivid imagination at work? An imaginary friend, perhaps? Or had the little girl glimpsed something—or someone—from the museum's haunted past?

Hide-and-Shriek

David McNair, the brother of Missouri's first governor, Alexander McNair, traveled from Pennsylvania in 1800 to settle in St. Charles. Around 1806, he built the red brick building at 724 South Main Street. He also constructed a stone circular lime kiln on the street and built St. Charles's first icehouse, where the community would store their perishable food.

After the War of 1812, McNair bought a ferry and repaired the boat landing off the Missouri River, which sat behind his home property.

This boat landing is where the Lewis & Clark Expedition stayed from May 16 to 21 in 1804. Here, they made final preparations before leaving to explore the Louisiana Territory and map a route to the Pacific Ocean.

Another famous person is associated with this structure. You might have heard of Abraham Lincoln? In the 1860s, the building served as his local presidential campaign headquarters. Perhaps Abraham Lincoln himself walked the rooms you stand in now.

In 2007, a student wrote to the owner of the building about a school field trip to the David McNair House. She inquired about ghosts. He responded confirming that the previous owner had spotted a short lady, approximately five feet tall, in a long 1800s period dress. The ghost could be seen through a set of glass shelves.

Currently, the building is known as Mad Hatter Antiques & More, which a local married couple has run for the past decade. Although a family member now lives in the second-floor apartment, that wasn't always the case. About eight years ago, it was vacant.

The first peculiar thing happened at this time: One of the items for sale in the first-floor's center room was a Boyds Bears Snowman. When the husband opened the store in the morning, the snowman had moved from its original place. The man would put it back where it belonged, only to find it in a different spot in the morning. This game of hide-and-seek went on for a time, until the owner decided to play his *own* game with the ghost. He removed the snowman from the shelf and marked it as NFS, not for sale. For fun, he hid the figurine for the ghost to find. Every morning, when he found the snowman somewhere different, he'd put it in a new hiding spot. The game still continues today. Can you find the snowman figurine in the store? Would you play hide-and-seek with a ghost?

Beyond the game, there were other signs of spooky activity. Some mornings,

when the couple opened the store, they would find crystal stone jewelry boxes opened and emptied. Thankfully, the jewelry hadn't been stolen, but pieces were placed around the shop. A music box playing "The Nutcracker" would echo throughout the rooms out of nowhere. Maybe a previous shopper had wound the crank and left the store before the music box began to play? Or maybe . . . it wasn't a customer at all.

When the couple started selling expensive merchandise, they installed motion detectors and alarms in the store. If the motion detector picked up any movement after hours, it would trigger the alarm and notify the police and owners. They'd meet at the store and investigate if someone had broken in and what had been stolen.

The owners felt secure with the additional alarm system, especially when it was activated the first night. Someone had traipsed through their store. The motion detectors picked up the perpetrator in the center room. The alarm sounded and police were dispatched to the scene. The husband met the police at the store. After they surveyed the interior and exterior of the building, they didn't see any signs of a burglary. Relieved that it was a false alarm, most likely from being a new system, they all went home.

Until it happened again.

And *again*.

For the next few weeks, the ritual continued. Each time, the alarm detected someone or something in the first-floor's center room. And each time, the police found no disturbances. What was triggering the same room's motion detectors, night after night? To this day, the owners still aren't quite sure.

To be safe, the husband has made it a habit to say "Good night, see you next week" when he leaves his weekly shift. A single strand of lights hangs across the middle room, glowing throughout the night. Even ghosts can be afraid of the dark, right?

Doomed Guests

The federal style three-story brick building with twin anchored chimneys at 700 South Main Street was built in 1805 and known as Farmer's Home or Farmer's Tavern. Missouri's First Governor, Alexander McNair, owned the building and ran it as a boarding house for state legislators when St. Charles served as the state's first capital from 1821 to 1826.

When travelers came through St. Charles, the inn and tavern were a favorite resting place. Lodging was $0.25 per night. For an additional $0.25, they could fill their bellies with cornbread and common fixings, believed to be wild game and fish, and for $0.375, they could upgrade to white bread and chicken fixings. The inn and saloon occupied the space for over a century.

In 1980, John Dengler and his wife, Selba Tru, purchased the home and restored it. Dengler ran his tobacconist store (a shop that sells tobacco products) on the first floor, while the second and third floors were living quarters. Through the years, he often shared the first floor with another business and housed a few renters upstairs.

With a building that's over two hundred years old, there are bound to be some terrifying tales. People might report phenomena like dolls turning and looking different directions on their own, objects floating in midair, and radios switching stations. Some insist the stories are folklore, passed down from generations. Based on their own experiences, others believe differently.

One of the tenants of a country wares store, Peggy, had a busy and frightening Saturday morning. Preparing her booth for the popular Festival of the Little Hills event in August, she made another trip up the staircase to the second-floor parlor to get more supplies. A light touch brushed her left shoulder and whispered in her ear.

"Peggy."

Unnerved, she tore down the stairs and into the store where she found Tru, one of the owners. Peggy explained that Tru's husband, Dengler, must be playing a trick on her. But Dengler wasn't in the store. He'd left to run an errand. Tru laughed and suggested a ghost had been the trickster.

After all, Tru had experienced her own ghosts in the building. She loved listening to 1120 KMOX on the radio. One afternoon, as she relaxed, the station switched to eerie symphonic music without anyone turning the dial. In the south parlor, she'd sometimes hear a baby cry and then a soothing gentleman's voice with a French accent. Though Dengler didn't believe in ghosts, he had theories about their identities. Once, a young mother lost her little girl while living in the building. And the Frenchman could be one of the original owners, Antoine Marechal.

Dengler's tobacco shop was in the same part of the building that once housed the ladies dining room. Oftentimes, the owner smelled the aroma of vegetables cooking, even though a kitchen no longer existed.

In 1982, Dengler's two daughters lived in the third-floor north bedroom. In the evenings, the sisters often stayed up chatting in their room before going to sleep. One night, alone in the house, strange noises startled them. They heard footsteps lumbering up and down the stairs, but only the two sisters were in the house. This happened twice a week around 10:00 p.m. Maybe they weren't alone after all.

A year later, another disturbing incident

occurred. One of the daughters and her grandma spent the night alone in the house. The daughter was in the second-floor kitchen while her grandma slept soundly in a nearby bedroom. When she pulled open the refrigerator to get a late-night snack, she heard a wicked cackle. She froze in horror. After ten seconds of the wretched noise, she slammed the door. The laughing stopped. Perhaps her grandma had gotten up to use the restroom? She tiptoed to her grandma's room, slipped the door open, and peeked inside. There was Grandma, asleep in her bed, snoring away.

Although the store is no longer a tavern or inn, perhaps the guests of long-ago didn't want their stay to end. If you look carefully in a certain light, you might just see them before they vanish into thin air . . . like a wisp of tobacco smoke.

Newbill-McElhiney House

Storybooks and Specters

Have you ever wanted to move somewhere new for a change of scenery? Do you think ghosts feel the same way? This one did.

Amanda is the owner of Once Upon a Time, a shop for lovers of storybooks, which first opened at 340 South Main Street. Once Upon a Time shared the building with Elements Herbology. Each morning when Amanda opened the store, she greeted the house; and every evening at closing time, she wished it a good night. She knew the history of the house and wanted to be kind in case she wasn't alone.

Long ago, when a family lived there, a little girl, Sara, died from an illness. The shop owner would see Sara playing peek-a-boo on the stairs leading to the basement. Sara's features reminded her of Alice in Wonderland. Amanda thought her shop, filled with storybook treasures, was the perfect place for the little girl. It seems that Sara agreed.

Amanda often played music over the store's speakers. One afternoon, though, she decided silence would be soothing after a busy day. Out of nowhere, the moment she turned the music off, the Mary Poppins soundtrack blasted suddenly through the store. Amanda was both startled *and* perplexed. Had she turned it on by accident? But that didn't make sense—she'd never chosen the Mary Poppins soundtrack before. Unless . . . could that have been little Sara, making herself known?

Over the years, Sara seemed happy with the store and Amanda. There was no reason to leave. However, it didn't remain that way.

The basement served as a stock room for employees—but they weren't alone. It seemed the ghost of a crotchety old man with a top hat had also made the basement his lair. Unlike other spirits who sometimes drift from room to room, this grumpy ghost never wandered upstairs. Since he saw the basement as his and his alone, he'd switch the lights on and off when employees visited to get items from the stock room. They complained of pounding headaches when they left, almost as if the old man was sending them a warning: "Stay out of my basement!"

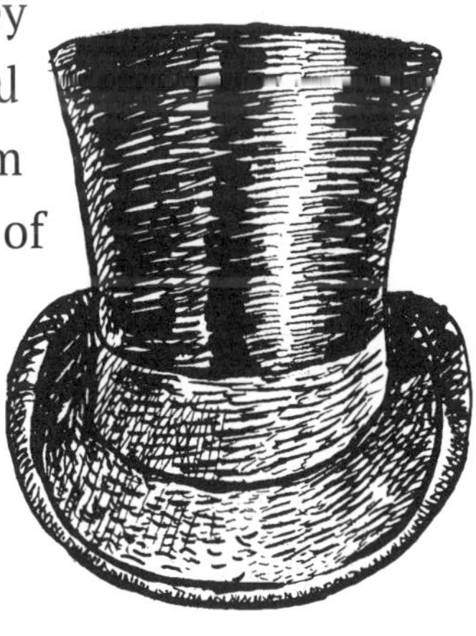

Though Amanda eventually moved her Once Upon a Time

shop up the street to a different location, the current owner of Aquarian Herbs at 340 South Main Street confirmed the male ghost still dwells in the basement. Rowdy noises from the second-floor's empty apartment also occasionally interrupt classes. When the noises first began, the shop owner contacted the landlord to find out if a tenant had moved in. As it turned out . . . the apartment was vacant.

Amanda moved her shop to the building at 625 South Main Street, the brick stand-alone building featuring many windows and a quaint, inviting porch with an awning, known as the Newbill-McElhiney House. She invited Sara to come along so she wouldn't have to stay with the mean basement dweller. Would Sara decide to move to a new home after all that time? Would you?

The Newbill-McElhiney House (the shop's new location for a couple of years) has a unique history of its own. Mill owner Franklin S. Newbill built the basement and ground floor of this brick house in 1836. Unfortunately, the mill failed only a few weeks later.

In 1840, a prominent psychiatrist, Dr. William J. McElhiney, purchased the house. Since he had a large family of a wife and twelve children, he expanded the home to include a second floor, as seen today. The family lived on the first and second floors and the doctor set up his practice in the basement, where he treated patients.

Following the move, Amanda settled the shop into the first floor of the house, elevated from the street. The stairs from the sidewalk lead to the front porch, which stretches across the majority of the windows and door. At times, Amanda thought she saw Sara out of the corner of her eye. But was it wishful thinking? Unsure if there were any ghosts in her new store or if the little girl had followed, she continued business as usual.

One day, a return customer from the previous building visited the new location. As she shopped the rooms filled with books, crystals, and jewelry, she saw an unexpected sight. It was Sara, the ghost of the little girl. The customer had recognized her from the previous location down the street! She excitedly shared the information with Amanda, saying Sara must have followed her to the new store.

Amanda felt a chill rush through her. How could the customer know this? Amanda had

whispered her invitation to Sara in private, with no one else around to hear. Perhaps some bonds—even those between the living and the dead—are stronger than we realize. And maybe Sara liked the idea of having twice as many visitors to watch over.

Chilling Cauldrons

Feeling a bit famished from all the ghost stories? Main Street specializes in savory bites and sweet treats. If you're looking for a restaurant where you can tame your hunger *and* unleash your spooky imagination, you've come to the right place.

Phantom Prankster

The sights and sounds that visitors have observed at this restaurant do not seem to be the work of a mean or evil ghost. More like a prankster trying to have some fun. What do you think?

In 1880, the 500 block of South Main Street was originally called the Tavern Block. The brick building of 501 served the village as part of William Eckert's Tavern complex, possibly as a livery stable, a place where horses could be cared for or rented out for the day. The original Eckert's Tavern sat to the rear of this building, behind the garden patio. (This stone building was even one of the sites considered for the first State Capitol when St. Charles was made the first capital of Missouri in 1820.) After the tavern complex, the building has changed ownership and been different businesses, including a manufacturing company, mattress factory, and winery. These days, the barbeque restaurant, Salt + Smoke, has moved in. The ghosts don't seem as active, but the stories remain alive.

Locals believe there are two ghosts, a man and a woman, who speak French. One night, after closing the restaurant, a past manager turned off all the second-floor lights before heading downstairs. When she realized she'd forgotten something, she went back upstairs and found all the lights on again. Had she simply misremembered turning the lights off? Or were the French-speaking spirits playing a joke on her?

She's not the only person to have had strange occurrences in the building. An upstairs door would open and close on its own. One woman reported they often used a fire extinguisher to keep the door propped open. Several times, she would jog downstairs to grab something, only to find the door closed when she returned to the server station. The fire extinguisher rested against the opposite wall. Certainly, one of her coworkers had shut the door. Not a chance. When she asked around, everyone confirmed no one had stepped foot upstairs. They had experienced similar incidents, too. How creepy!

Once, another server stood at the counter rolling utensils in napkins for the next day. Suddenly, the tray of clean silverware crashed onto the floor! The server glanced up to see if a coworker had brushed past the counter and accidently bumped the tray. But no—the server was all alone in the room. Or was he?

Sometimes, the silverware is stolen from its normal spot, only to return later in unusual places. Doors swing open for no reason upstairs, and sometimes people hear a couple arguing in French. Witnesses find boxes in the storage area strewn about, as if there's been a rowdy fight. People say the ghosts are most active between 11:00 p.m. and 1:00 a.m. They seem to enjoy playing in the front bar area where they spill wine, rearrange glasses, and move things around. I guess that's one way to keep the bartenders and servers on their toes!

Who could these ghosts have been in their former lives? The old St. Borromeo Cemetery in the neighboring block of 400 South Main Street may hold the answers. When the town moved the graveyard generations ago, many believe they forgot some of the bodies, causing the spirits to run restless. Wherever these prankster ghosts may have come from, they seem to have no intention of leaving!

Distraught Dinner Guests

Thirsty for more? Wander north a few blocks until you come to First Capitol. The three-story brick building with a balcony on the corner at 217 South Main Street has been standing since the early 1800s. The structure has a storied history, as it's been a home or business for over two hundred years. Candy, beef, biscuits, and paint were once sold at this location—quite an assortment!

In the 1890s, a couple loved their home so much they reportedly decided to stay forever! Rumor has it a man and a woman have been spotted on the landing of the stairs leading to the second floor. Which shouldn't be odd as it's been a restaurant for over forty years. But these aren't your typical customers. The man's handlebar moustache and clothes from another century tend to stick out. And although the woman's face is a mystery, her long, dark hair complements her red dress. In the midst of a busy day, the couple will turn around on the landing and disappear into the wall where there once was a doorway.

Apparently, the two prefer a quiet atmosphere. When the televisions play a sporting event and the crowd gets too loud, the screens will suddenly shut off, as if in disapproval. Although nobody has found a clear reason for the interruption, St. Charles locals know the truth: the ghosts who call this building home simply like their peace and quiet.

Beyond the phantom couple, an anonymous employee confirmed another haunting presence—a ghostly little girl. One evening after closing, as he carried the trash through the darkened restaurant, he saw a little girl crying behind the bar. To his shock, when he moved closer, she vanished! Despite sharing his experience with coworkers, no one else has heard or seen the mysterious child. What do you think? Was the ghostly girl a result of weary eyes after a long day's work? Or does the historic building harbor more spirits than even St. Charles locals suspect?

A long-time employee from 1985 to 2012 experienced her own goosebumps one day. She headed down to the basement, where the staff kept supplies and a copier. Needing to make copies, she powered on the machine and went to work. As she waited, chills crawled up her neck. You know when you get that feeling that someone is staring at you? Although she didn't feel threatened, she had the eerie feeling she wasn't alone. The woman figured another employee had come down to use the supplies in the basement.

When she looked up from the copy machine, she spotted a wavy shadow near the original stone wall. Taking a deep breath, she decided to look closer. Who did she find? Not a soul. Although this only happened to her once, the experience still haunts her today.

A previous manager arrived at the restaurant early one day to set up for an event they were having on the second floor. Since he was alone, he blasted the music on the two Bose speakers, enjoying the tunes. But maybe he wasn't the only one in the restaurant after all. According to him, one of the speakers flew suddenly across the room. Familiar with the building's spooky reputation, the manager chalked it up to the ghosts being angry with his music choice or its volume. Was it the man with the handlebar moustache or the faceless woman in the red dress? Visit the restaurant for yourself and tell your friends what you see.

THE
MOTHER-IN-
LAW HOUSE
FIRST BRICK
DOUBLE HOUSE
BUILT
1866

Resilient Relative

Have you ever lived with a relative like a grandpa or aunt? This family did—but their relative never left, not even after death.

Built in 1866, the house at 500 South Main Street is known as the first double house, or duplex, in St. Charles. Mill owner Francis Kremer built the house for himself and his young bride, who desperately missed her mother. Kremer didn't want his wife to be sad and homesick. He found the solution by building a house with two doors. Both sides were identical, with a wall down the middle. The right side housed the family, while the left side welcomed Kremer's mother-in-law.

It was a perfect solution—or so they thought. As the story goes, the mother-in-law could often be found on her side of the house alone, bored, and rocking in her chair while staring out the window.

The mother-in-law's granddaughter, Donna Hafer, transformed the historic home into a restaurant, which she ran for many years and fittingly named "Mother-In-Law House." Also fitting, it appears that the mother-in-law's spirit lingered on. While the restaurant was in operation, eerie occurrences often happened on the side of the restaurant where she once lived. Glasses and utensils disappeared with no explanation. Coffee cups toppled over and dump their contents into guests' laps. Water glasses inexplicably spilled. Dinnerware floated through the air. And food mysteriously changed temperature.

Not knowing how to make the charades end, the granddaughter decided to redecorate that part of the building. (Previously, she had decorated the restaurant to match the 1850-1900 era of the home's previous residents, removing the dividing wall but leaving the vertical wooden beams as they were.) After the redecoration, the ghost remained but seemed happier. For good measure, the employees closed the restaurant in the evenings by saying, "Mother-in-law, we love you."

Customers often requested table 1, the mother-in-law's table, hoping to dine with her spirit. Others would arrive as the first guests of the day, only to insist someone was sitting there already (even if that someone was invisible). Old Victorian relics are stored in the building and one, in particular, is interesting: an antique funeral box filled with delicate yarn flowers. Victorian funerals during the winter months often used wreaths of yarn flowers since fresh flowers were difficult to find. Since it was common to have wakes in family homes during the 1800s, this relic isn't out of place. Could this box have been used at the mother-in-law's funeral?

When the granddaughter sold the restaurant, the new owner changed its name to Thompkins Restaurant after its crossroad, Thompkins Street. In May 2023, the restaurant was sold again and renamed The Main House. During the sale, the former owner refused to go into the building by herself, still haunted by memories of unearthly events.

Today, the current Main House owner isn't afraid of the dark or ghosts. But certain happenings have made him wonder. One summer evening, with the front door propped open, he began closing duties behind the bar. As he counted the cash and tapped information into the computer, he suddenly sensed someone behind him. Figuring it was a patron who wanted to order food, he turned around to greet them—only to find nothing but the open doorway. He looked around the room and even checked the mirror to see if he'd missed a customer. But again . . . not a soul. Perhaps the mother-in-law still fancies her favorite table, more than a century and a half later.

A group of guests came in to dine and were seated at a four-top table against the back wall under the eagle portrait. One of the women took the seat facing the mother-in-law's table and favorite window. While their group studied the menu, someone pushed the woman's chair in toward the table. She turned around to the thank the server but no one was there.

Even with all the ghostly activity in the dining room, the *creepiest* incidents happened in the basement wine cellar. Wooden crates filled with wine bottles line the walls. On February 7, 2024, an employee took inventory and carefully removed wine bottles from their cases. Out of nowhere, from the opposite wall, bottles of red wine hurdled off the top shelf. One. Two. Three. The worker tried to process the situation as seven bottles shattered to the floor, spilling blood-red liquid everywhere. Recovering from the shock just in time, he managed to catch the eighth bottle mid-air.

When the employee told the owner what had happened, they reviewed the footage from the security camera together. The owner assumed those particular bottles had fallen because their curved shaped made them unstable on the shelves. When he replaced the broken bottles in the cellar, he adjusted their position so they wouldn't fall again.

Two months later, on April 11, in a vacant wine cellar, the event repeated. Eight bottles of the same brand of red wine appeared to jump off the shelf and smash on the floor. Don't believe it? The Main House owner has both incidents captured on security footage with date stamps to prove it. Since then, that particular red wine has found a new home—securely in their original boxed cases. After all, one can never be too careful with ghosts lurking around.

Protective Spirit

When you cross Thompkins Street, you'll see a fire-glazed brick building at 426 South Main Street, currently home to European Accents. However, throughout its history, this building has served as a saloon, catholic church, orphanage, and a soft drink company. Constructed in 1808-1809 and reconstructed in 1855, this location offered prime real estate, as Thompkins Street was the main street for traveling carriages. (And maybe ghosts, as well?)

During one of the building's many renovations over the years, workers made a chilling discovery. For decades, people often reported the sound of a baby's cry echoing through the walls. After searching the place, no children were ever found on the premises. They couldn't find an explanation, until the workers took down a wall during renovations and found the source of those haunting sounds. In between the pieces of drywall, a crib laid abandoned.

Once a church, the pulpit sat where the beginning of the stairs is today. Poor parishioners took their services from the first floor, and the rich took theirs from the second floor. It's on the second floor where the current owners met the "protective angel" for the first time.

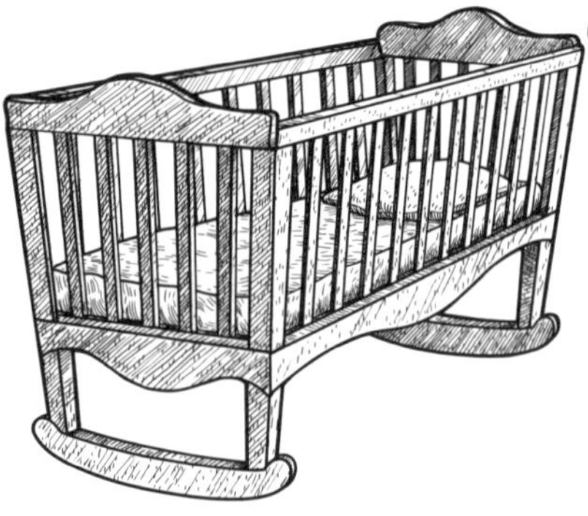

The couple bought and opened their store, European Accents, in

2005. But before they opened their doors, they spruced up the place. One day, the husband and their Italian greyhound were alone in the store, hard at work. Perched on a large ladder propped against the second-floor wall, he painted around the small window. Suddenly, something knocked the man over—and the ladder toppled with him! But instead of tumbling to the staircase below, both the man and ladder landed on the second-story floor. On its way down, the ladder banged against the railing, leaving marks indented in the wood that visitors can still see today.

Oddly enough, the owner sustained no injuries. His glasses fell off, but amazingly, not only did the paint not spill, the man still clutched the paint brush in his hand. Sprawled on the floor, the owner tried to get his bearings. Then, suddenly, he heard a whisper.

"*Gordy.*"

Three times he heard the name, getting louder each time.

The man lay stunned. Gordy was his nickname, but only close family and friends used it. But he was alone with his dog. Could this be the voice of the protective angel others had heard?

Gordy's greyhound thought so. The dog often raced up and down the stairs of the second floor, as if playing with someone. In those days, the shop had no customers. No living customers, that is. At the end of the day, when it was time to go home, the dog reluctantly left his friend.

These two weren't the only ones to experience mysteries on the second-floor. The previous owner had organized her shop with boys' clothes on one side of the room and girls' on the other. Yet, when she opened the store many mornings, she'd find they had been swapped overnight—boys' stuff on the girls' side and girls' stuff on the boys'. What in the world?

And of course, the basement has its own resident ghost. (What creepy basement doesn't?) It's said a little boy in a brown coat haunts the storeroom closest to the stairs. Although the basement is for employees only, the shop's second-floor inhabitant seems eager for visitors—perhaps to introduce you to his basement-dwelling friend. Listen closely as you shop; those footsteps overhead might be inviting you to discover what lurks in the shadows below.

Grandma's Cookies on Main Street

Goosebumps at Grandma's

The smell of fresh baked cookies doesn't just attract people strolling down the sidewalk. It also summons the dead. In 1818, Father Charles Felix Van Quickenborne owned the property at 401 South Main Street, building a priest's residence and armory of handmade brick. Behind the building was the Catholic Cemetery. For the last nearly fifty years, the family of founder, Charlotte Thompson, has been tempting tourists and residents with their delicious cookies at the location.

One employee who has worked at Grandma's Cookies for thirteen years says a few ghosts have made the bakery their home. One day, during store hours, the employee was working in the kitchen when she heard a little boy's giggle coming from the front storeroom, where customers browse and purchase displayed cookies. The employee figured a family had come in to buy a treat, so she paused what she was doing and headed for the storeroom. As she made her way out of the kitchen, she heard the giggle again. But when she came into the store, she stopped short. Not a single person, adult or child, waited in the store. Maybe a family had changed their minds, decided not to buy any cookies, and walked out? Only . . . both doors were closed. She had heard the giggle not just once, but twice. With dozens of chocolate chip and sugar cookies on display, can you blame the little boy ghost for giggling with excitement?

Apparently, on the second floor, a rambunctious ghost named John lives in the current storage room, which was a bedroom at one time. Employees often hear things crashing around up there, even though nobody is upstairs. Another ghost, Sarah, wears a black dress and stands by the stoves and bathroom on the first floor. Perhaps she's keeping a watchful eye on customers as they pass by?

A couple of other bizarre occurrences have taken place in the back rooms of the main level. Several employees have witnessed a little white dress floating across the room on its own. And earlier this year, the workers took a picture of another unexplained event. While one woman packed cookie orders for shipping in the back room and the rest of the crew made cookies in the mixing room, they suddenly heard the loud crash of shattering glass erupting from the kitchen. The group in the mixing room, figuring their coworker had moved to the kitchen, called out to ask if she was all right. When she told them she was in the back room, a hush fell over the group. Not a soul was working in the kitchen.

Together, they decided to investigate. When they nervously entered the kitchen, they immediately noticed something odd. On the floor in front of the sink sat three plastic bowls, lined up in a row, right-side up. Normally, these bowls were stacked *beside* the sink. How did the bowls end up on the floor? There were no windows or doors open, so it couldn't have been the wind. Maybe an employee had snuck into the kitchen to spook the others? But when? They'd all been together the entire time. And besides, how had they all heard the sound of glass breaking when the bowls were made of plastic? Nothing else in the kitchen was broken, nor out of place. Although they took a picture to capture the sight of the three mysterious bowls, simply hearing the eerie tale is enough to make the hairs on your arm stand up. It seems the ghostly boy may not be the only spirit with a sweet tooth in this historic St. Charles bakery.

Whispering Graves

Did you know there was an old, forgotten cemetery tucked between these shops and restaurants on Main Street in St. Charles? Peek outside the window behind Grandma's Cookies store. Do you see the log building and plot of land? You're looking at an old cemetery. Although most of the graves were moved to another location, it's rumored that several bodies were left behind.

On the banks of the Missouri River in 1769, Louis Blanchette, the founder of St. Charles, and his French-Canadian travelers set up their settlement. Since many early residents of St. Charles were both French and Catholic, they wanted a place to worship. They added a rough log cabin to their settlement for Mass and church gatherings. Today, the Lewis and

Clark Statue in Frontier Park marks the area of the original church. Like rivers sometimes do, the Missouri River continued to flood, so they moved the church up the hill.

If you search behind the shop at 401 South Main and Jackson Streets, you'll find a vertical (*poteaux en terre)* log structure. The original church was moved to this site. The current log structure mimics the area's first church, San Carlos Borromeo, in 1791. Supposedly, Lewis and Clark and their traveling party attended Mass here on May 20, 1804, before beginning the Corps of Discovery. They'd arrived in St. Charles a few days prior to gather supplies for the journey up the Missouri River.

The site wasn't only a church. The remains of Louis Blanchette and his wife were once buried underground beneath the church. And they weren't the only bodies. (That's right—the area you are standing on was once an eighteenth century graveyard!) One grave, in particular, seems to have a resident that can't rest in peace.

In 1822, a young St. Charles woman of twenty-three years old gave birth to a baby boy. Sadly, after she brought her son into the world, she developed a fever. She prayed the intense love of her son would overpower the illness and she would recover. Unfortunately, her health deteriorated, and she died. The day

of her passing, sick and delirious, she managed to ask for a priest to sit with her in her last moments.

The poor woman only owned one nice dress, so her grieving family dressed her in her wedding gown for her funeral. The Lady in White was laid to rest at St. Charles Borromeo Cemetery. Visitors claim that if you wait quietly in the cemetery at dusk as the sun sets, the Lady in White might appear. Some say they've seen her in the corner kneeling, as if in prayer.

The graveyard once had hundreds of headstones marking the graves of early settlers. But look around—do you see any? In the 1850s, when officials established a new St. Charles Borromeo Cemetery two miles northwest, workers carefully unearthed and moved the bodies to the new cemetery. That is . . . they moved the bodies they could find.

Archaeological digs and foundation work over the years have discovered human remains left behind. In 1917, the owner of the Farmer's

Home building across the street witnessed unbelievable findings. A construction crew dug into the hillside behind the corner armory building. The owner couldn't believe his eyes. The men discovered a large number of bodies that hadn't been removed. At another site, a new building's floor was being laid and the crew found a rather shocking surprise: a cluster of forgotten bones encased in a hunk of concrete.

Crews also discovered pieces of men's clothing resembling the French style from over two hundred years ago. The old graveyard once spread across what has become the entire 400 block of South Main Street. Local historians believe more than fifty bodies may still lie buried beneath these buildings today. So while you shop for a gift or eat your lunch, remember that the ground under your feet is filled with skeletons. Watch your step!

Petrified Pottery

The three-story building at 330 South Main Street has an intriguing past. As one of the buildings known as "Stone Row," it was built in 1820 with hand-cut Burlington limestone. At first, a post office operated on the main floor. The postman also worked as a tailor, so he set up his tailor shop upstairs. A decade later, the building became an extension of the jail housing nonviolent criminals. After fifteen to twenty years, the building primarily became a residence. Since there were two separate entrances, one family lived on the main floor and another on the second floor. Can you imagine your house once being a jail?

Fast forward to May 2012 when the current owner, Katheryne, rented the place for her Siostra Polish Pottery shop. Although thrilled by her decision, there was much work to do. When the previous owner, Bob, passed away in 2017, Katheryne purchased the building. Bob had been a furniture upholster and stored his inventory of chairs and fabrics upstairs in the attic. She dismissed previous warnings about hauntings and focused instead on opening her shop. How bad could it be? With everything she had to do ahead of the opening, Katheryne didn't have time to sell any of the old furniture in the attic and figured she would deal with it later.

Within a year, strange things started to happen. A customer came into the shop and warned Katheryne to watch out for Sarah, a female ghost in a dress who hurried from the office to the stairs. He also described a male ghost, possibly Sarah's husband, relaxing in a chair while staring at a small black and white television in the corner. Finally, the man told Katheryne he'd seen ghostly children playing around the store. Katheryne listened to the customer but hadn't seen or felt anything herself.

The following year, while visiting the Irish shop down the street, she met a lady who claimed to sense spirits. In fact, the moment the lady laid eyes on Katheryne, her eyes grew as big as saucers—apparently, Katheryne had an invisible companion standing next to her! After discussing ghosts and how her pottery store was supposedly haunted, the woman insisted she come investigate herself.

Having never set foot in her store, she was delighted by more than the hand-painted stoneware. She, too, saw Sarah bustling around the first floor and told Katheryne she better stay out of her way—the ghost had work to do. Amazed that two customers had now seen the same thing, Katheryne thought it might be a coincidence. But then the women asked a startling question: "Bob wants to know what you're going to do with all the chairs in the attic?"

Katheryne was almost speechless. How could this woman know about the chairs in the attic—not to mention Bob's name—if she had never been in the store?

Later that same day, while straightening cups and mugs, Katheryne's heart suddenly began to race. A heavy pressure crushed her torso, making it hard to breathe. Katheryne had an overwhelming urge to move. Once she stepped back toward the register, the heavy sensation disappeared.

One chilly January day, Katheryn heard what sounded like a marble dropping, bouncing a few times, and then rolling across the floor upstairs. But the second floor was empty—how could this be? She tried to forget about it, but then it happened a second and a third time. Enough was enough. She decided to investigate the second floor but found nothing. Completely freaked out and not wanting to spend another minute there, she rushed downstairs and closed the store early.

Two years later, in the spirit of Siostra, which means sister, Katheryne's own sister and family came to visit. They stayed in the second-floor apartment for their summer vacation. While working at the kitchen table one day, Katheryne's sister accidently dropped her pencil on the floor, where it rolled under the furnace. Annoyed, the sister got on her hands and knees, searching for the pencil. Thankfully, she found it—along with another discovery.

Marbles.

Thinking nothing of it and figuring they wouldn't be missed, she threw the dust-covered marbles in the trash. But she had made a grave mistake. In an instant, all the lights in the apartment began to flicker and then went completely out. Strange.

The sister went downstairs and asked Katheryne where the extra lightbulbs were stored.

"The lights all went out," said the sister.

"What do you mean?" said Katheryne.

The sister explained how she dropped her pencil, it rolled under the furnace, and she found it along with some marbles.

Katheryne's eyebrows rose. "Marbles?"

"Yeah."

"What did you do with them?"

"I threw them in the trash."

Convinced the ghostly children were upset her sister had thrown out their toy, Katheryne told her to put the marbles back. As soon as she did, all the apartment lights flickered back on. Can you guess where the marbles are today?

Still buried under the furnace, left untouched.

The classroom adjacent to the apartment on the second floor may also have a resident ghost. A gentleman in a suit and bowler hat paces between the two windows and door that lead to the balcony facing Main Street. If you're lucky, you may just spot him looking out one window to see what's happening outside, before pacing to the next. Katheryne herself has heard footsteps from this room. Although she doesn't know his name, he does make his presence known by sometimes unplugging lamps when no one else but her is in the shop.

He is particularly fond of the holidays. The timers for the Christmas lights will malfunction. Katheryne times them to come on in the evening and turn off in the daytime. The lights twinkle on as planned but won't turn off with the rising sun. Even when she buys new timers to replace the malfunctioning ones, the same thing happens. It's hard to blame anyone for wanting the Christmas lights on all the time, don't you agree?

One evening, the owner of Bella Vino, the restaurant across the street from Siostra Polish Pottery, worked in her office upstairs. As she glanced out the window at the charming street, something caught her eye. In the second-floor window of the pottery store, she saw a man. Wiping her eyes clear from the busy day, she checked again—there he was peering out the window!

Unsure whether she should call the police, she quickly searched for Katheryne's phone number. When she couldn't find it, she glanced up again at the window. To her relief, the man was gone. Maybe her eyes were playing tricks on her after a long day at the restaurant? She decided to go home and get some much-needed sleep.

But the next morning, the woman couldn't shake her worry that someone actually *had* broken into her neighbor's store. She waited on the sidewalk for Katheryne before the shop opened, and together, they searched the exterior for any signs of a break-in. Nothing.

Inside, they found no sign of any disturbance. No cash stolen. No products missing. And when they checked the second floor, all seemed well. Until Katheryne asked one crucial question: What did the man look like at the window?

"He wore a suit," the woman replied. "And a bowler hat."

The next time you pass by Siostra Polish Pottery, glance up at that second-floor window. The figure watching you isn't some intruder who broke in . . . he's someone who never left.

Native Traditions Gallery
STOP

Creepy Caller

Native Traditions Gallery is the home of beautiful Native American and Wildlife Art. Currently, the gallery can be found at 310 South Main Street, although that wasn't always the case. In 1988, a couple opened the gallery's first location at 612 South Main Street. After around eight years, they moved to 142 North Main Street. Why are these three different locations important? Because the same spine-tingling scenario happened at each one!

Eager to open their new gallery, the couple got to work one evening. With all the doors closed and locked, the original owners and current owner went down to the basement to organize inventory. Unlike other stores, this basement still had a dirt floor and the common limestone walls. An old cutout of a tunnel shaped hole, leading in the direction of the Missouri River, had been filled. Surrounded by creepy vibes, the telephone rang. *BRRRING!*

Who would be calling at this late hour? The wife started upstairs to answer the phone—but it stopped ringing. Figuring it must have been a wrong number, they continued working.

Keep in mind, before cell phones, we had

rotary phones, which couldn't be moved from one location to another. Phones were either installed on the wall or placed on a desktop in a cradle. If someone happened to forget to hang up when their call was finished, the phone company alerted the customer with an annoying alarm tone.

When the couple finished their projects for the night and came upstairs, they were shocked to hear an alarm blaring through the phone.

BEEP-BEEP-BEEP-BEEP.

The blue rotary phone was off the hook, laying on the counter, as if someone had answered the earlier call but then forgotten to hang up. But who? The husband and wife were all alone in the gallery . . . weren't they?

Eight years later, the gallery moved their artwork and blue rotary phone to 142 North Main Street, a bigger building with more showroom space. After store hours, the couple decided to get some extra work done. While the husband visited the restroom, his wife worked in the back office. Though the office had its own phone, the infamous blue rotary phone remained at the front counter.

BRRRING!

Hearing the sudden ring, the woman rose from her chair and made her way to the wall phone. Before she reached it, the ringing stopped.

When her husband returned, he immediately asked who had called.

"No one," she told him.

Not believing her, he asked again.

She explained that she hadn't even answered the phone—it had simply stopped ringing.

Why wouldn't her husband believe her story? When he passed the front counter to meet his wife in the back office, the blue rotary phone was off the hook. *Again*.

When the gallery moved to its third and final location of 310 South Main Street, what do you think happened? Around 2005, while training a new employee, the owner shared the unnerving stories about the blue rotary phone—now perched on the front counter.

While she spoke, as if on cue, the phone suddenly rang. But not the normal ring. No, it was an odd, electric sounding ring. Both women jumped at the eerie, jolting sound. The employee picked up the phone but heard nothing but silence—how strange! For the rest of the day, no matter how many times they tried using it, the blue phone stayed silent.

They called a phone repairman who came to check what was wrong. After testing all the wires and connections, he scratched his head. All the phone lines were fine. He wasn't sure how, but something had definitely fried the blue rotary phone—it never worked again. Maybe whoever—or *whatever*—had been making those mystery calls finally decided to hang up for good!

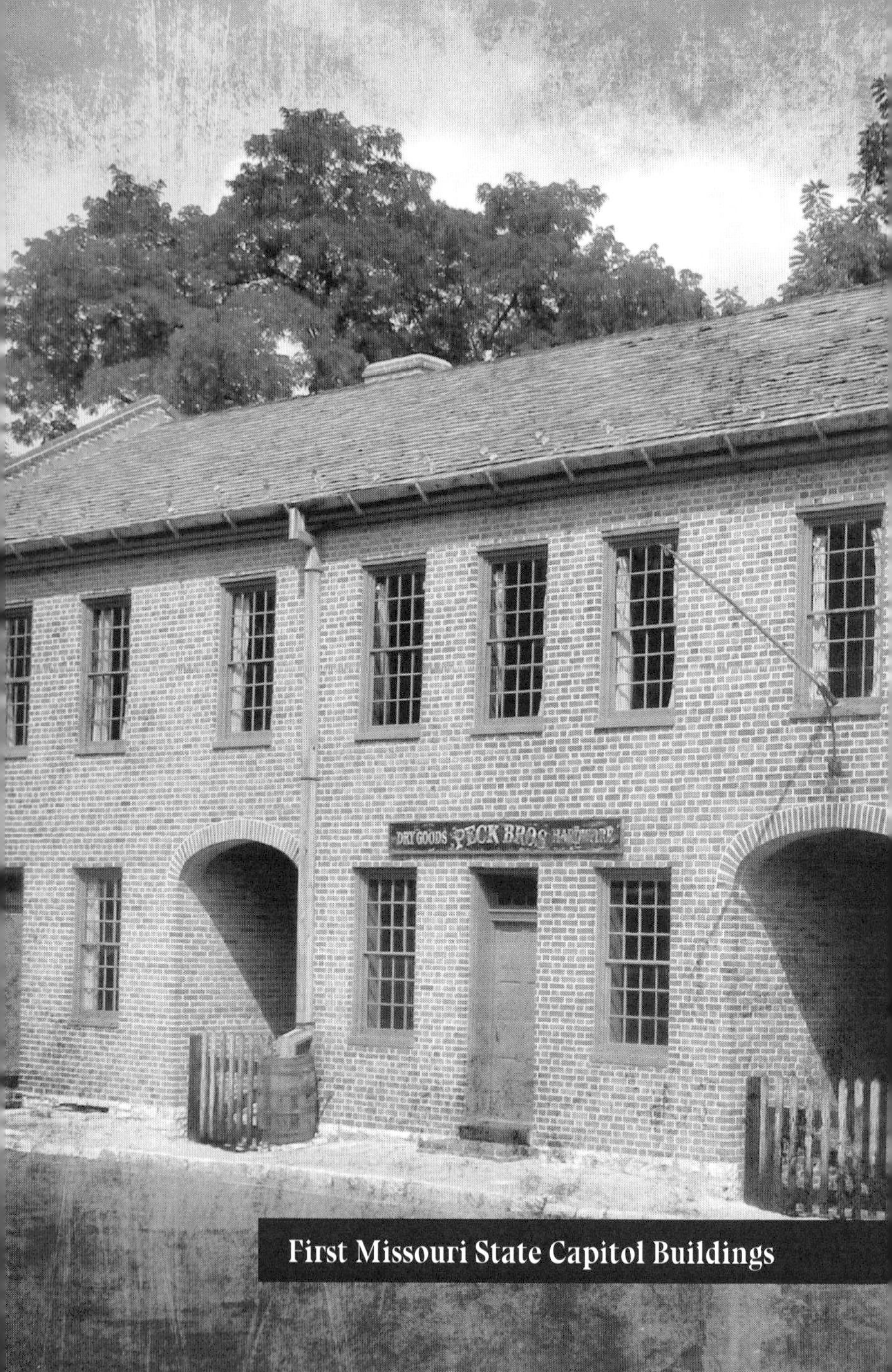

First Missouri State Capitol Buildings

Echoes From the Past

You look like you've seen a ghost. Have these stories buried you yet? Look alive, you don't want to miss these last bizarre and bone-chilling tales. You must stalk down the street to get from one site to the other. Get going! You don't have eternity.

Freaky First

We all know the state capital of Missouri is Jefferson City. However, until the Capitol building could be constructed, legislators needed a place to meet. Nine cities competed to host the state's temporary seat of government. The cities included Ste. Genevieve, St. Louis, St. Charles, Potosi, Florissant, Herculaneum, Cote Sans Dessein (extinct), Franklin, and Boonville. With a growing trade center located on the Missouri River and offering free meeting space, the decision was made. On November 25, 1820, Governor Alexander McNair signed a bill making St. Charles the first capital of Missouri.

The two adjoining Federal-style brick buildings at 200 South Main Street were owned by separate people. The Peck brothers, Charles and Ruluff, housed a general store and Ruluff's family residence on the first floor of one building. Next door, a man named Chauncy Shepard owned and operated his carpenter shop on the main floor. Upstairs, important government business happened! The second floor held special rooms where lawmakers met—the Senate and House chambers, the governor's office, and a small meeting room. Can you imagine all those important decisions being made right above a regular shop?

A team of archaeologists looked at the buildings in 1963 and thought part of them might have been used as an ice house where people stored food to keep it cold before refrigerators were invented. The larger part might have been a summer kitchen or stable. Since the street numbers have changed so many times over the past two hundred years, it's difficult to pinpoint exactly who lived and died in and around these buildings. But we *do* know that before the state acquired the land, people used the ground floor as shops and store fronts, and made their homes upstairs on the second-floor. In fact, some say a few of those long-ago residents never really left!

Sadly, Ruluff Peck died as a young man in 1828. We don't

know when he was born, but he got married in 1820 and his youngest son was only seven months old when he passed. The other building owner, Chauncey Shepard, had a tragic end, too. In 1840, he was harvesting ice from the frozen river with his two sons when he fell through the ice and drowned.

With so many people passing away in and near the property, it's no wonder the buildings give off chilling vibes, especially after dark! Employees speak of strange noises that seem to come from nowhere. Since there's no insulation between the two floors, it's easy to hear every creek and footstep—yes, even ghostly footsteps! Doors tend to pop open even when they've been latched. A couple of times in the Governor's office upstairs, people have heard the sound of someone opening the door and walking into the legislature. But when they go to inspect, there's no one there.

To keep with the building's historical feel, special battery-operated remote-controlled candles light the way instead of modern light bulbs. Occasionally, employees will find those candles glowing randomly, even when nobody has turned them on! Sometimes, in a chandelier with many candles, a single candle will mysteriously light up on its own.

Could Peck or Shepard still be "checking in" on their property after all these years? Visit the First State Capitol and find out for yourself.

Caskets and Cupboards

Last time you visited a furniture store, did they also sell caskets? In the nineteenth and early twentieth centuries, it was common for furniture makers to also specialize in funeral caskets. The Steinbrinker Furniture and Funeral Parlor once dwelled at 305 North Main Street, down the street from the First Capitol.

In 1900, workers built the north section of the building. The south section didn't come along until 1924, after the demolition of the old Monroe House Hotel. For much of the twentieth century, two brothers named John H. and Edward Steinbecker ran a very unusual business here—part furniture store, part funeral home.

As a certified undertaker, Edward Steinbrinker prepared dead bodies for burial or cremation and helped families make funeral arrangements. Besides selling furniture, rugs, and linoleum flooring, caskets were offered as well. And not just wooden caskets, but state-of-the-art metallic caskets and burial vaults. Their funeral services included everything a grieving family needed: preserving the body through a process called embalming, grave digging, and providing transportation to

burial sites. Can you imagine shopping for a new living room couch in the same place where families said goodbye to their loved ones? No wonder some people think spirits might still linger in these walls . . .

During the Victorian era, mourning traditions were different than they are today. Wakes, a gathering of family and friends to watch over the body before the funeral, often took place in the home of the deceased. There were three distinct morning periods: deep or full mourning, second mourning, and half-mourning. Each period had a specific length of time depending on your relationship with the deceased. Other rules included specific clothing, jewelry, colors, and more. You were considered immoral or dishonoring to the deceased if you didn't follow these rules.

Victorians were also very superstitious. They believed if you didn't stop the clock in a death room, you would have bad luck. And they warned that if you didn't hold your breath while going by a graveyard, you wouldn't get a proper burial when your time came!

By the early 1900s, when the Victorian era had ended, many families preferred having wakes at funeral parlors instead of their homes. Mr. Steinbrinker saw this change and added funeral services to his furniture business. The

front half of the building featured a showcase of chairs, tables, wardrobes, and more. The funeral parlor did business and services in the back half of the store.

Over four decades, the Steinbrinker family helped lay to rest many citizens of St. Charles. Eventually, they sold the business to the well-known Hackmann-Baue Company. Though the building later housed offices and a bar, today it stands empty and abandoned. Perhaps the thoughts of grave diggers and caskets scare people away. Does it scare you?

Enchanting Educator

About a mile and a half west, on a hill overlooking downtown St. Charles and the Missouri River, sits the five hundred-acre campus of Lindenwood University. With thousands of students from all over the United States and around the world, the college has grown immensely from its humble beginning.

The college was founded in 1832 by Mary Easton Sibley, the daughter of St. Louis's first postmaster, and her husband, George Sibley. Married at fifteen years old, Mary lived with her husband who was stationed at Fort Osage in western Missouri by Kansas City. During this time, Mary taught the children of the fort. Once Sibley completed his time in the military, the couple settled in St. Charles.

Sibley purchased the property in 1814, when Fort Osage was shut down for a period during the War of 1812. The large hill on the land was the perfect spot for Mary to build a school. The college name of Lindenwood came from the linden trees that covered the area. The big log cabin, known as The Lindenwood School of Girls, became the first college for women west of the Mississippi River.

Sibley Hall was the school's first residence hall and also the home of the school President, Rev. Addison Van Court Schenck, and his family. When it was used as a dormitory, many residents claimed to hear noises echoing from the empty rooms. Upon investigation, they found no cause for the strange sounds. As a music lover, Mary enjoyed playing her piano, which is now stored in the resident's hall. Some have reported hearing musical tunes being played in this very room.

One summer, Sibley Hall was emptied due to renovations. For safety reasons, the workmen locked all the doors while inside. But one day, as they busied themselves on the main level, the men heard sounds from above: female voices chattering, doors opening and closing, and the noise of an object being dragged across the floor. How was this possible? Doors had been secured and locked all day. The building had been evacuated prior to construction.

Confused, several men scrambled up the stairs. The workday was over, and they wanted to make sure that the ladies who had somehow gotten into the building could leave safely. When they searched the upper floors, they were completely vacant. Although not everyone agrees about the workmen story, many who spend time in this building tell the same tale—strange sounds echoing through empty hallways, disembodied footsteps, doors closing in distant rooms, and eerie whispers that send shivers up visitors' spines.

Mysterious noises aren't the only strange things happening in Sibley Hall. The building has a grand open staircase that rises up through all three floors. One day, a young woman hurried down those stairs, rushing to get to her next class. In her haste, she tripped and tumbled over the balcony. Surely, she'd be injured when she finally reached the bottom. Just in time, however, she felt something catch her from behind. A pair of gentle, strong hands stopped her fall. Shaken but relieved, she turned around to thank whoever had saved her—but her rescuer had vanished.

Word of the rescue on the stairs spread quickly across campus. Students began to believe that Mary Sibley herself had saved the young woman. After all, the school's founder had promised to always watch over her students.

The legend says every Halloween night, Mary Sibley returns to her school. Some say she walks from her grave in Lindenwood's cemetery, while others say she rides across campus on her horse. Either way, she always makes her way to Sibley Hall.

One year, a student wanted to bring this legend to life. She dressed up in old-fashioned clothes like Mary would have worn and reenacted the walk to the hall, frightening her friends. Once inside, she headed to the piano, just as Mary would have in life. But the student wasn't alone. Looking up, she saw a woman in a period dress standing with her back turned. At first, she thought it was just one of her friends trying to scare her. But when the mysterious woman slowly turned around, the student gasped—the face staring back at her was Mary Sibley! The student's terrified scream echoed in the room until she fainted dead away.

People say Mary Sibley promised her students that she would always watch over them, bringing good luck. Today, Mary rests with her family in the small cemetery

on campus overlooking a pond on the hill across from Hunter Stadium. Although only twenty-nine gravestones are marked, the cemetery is the resting place of thirty-four people and three dogs. Almost all these graves are from the 1800s.

Perhaps you can visit the graveyard or Sibley Hall and see for yourself if the legend is true. If you hear ghostly piano music playing or glimpse a woman in old-fashioned clothes watching from a window—it might just be Mary Sibley, keeping her promise. Do you dare find out for yourself?

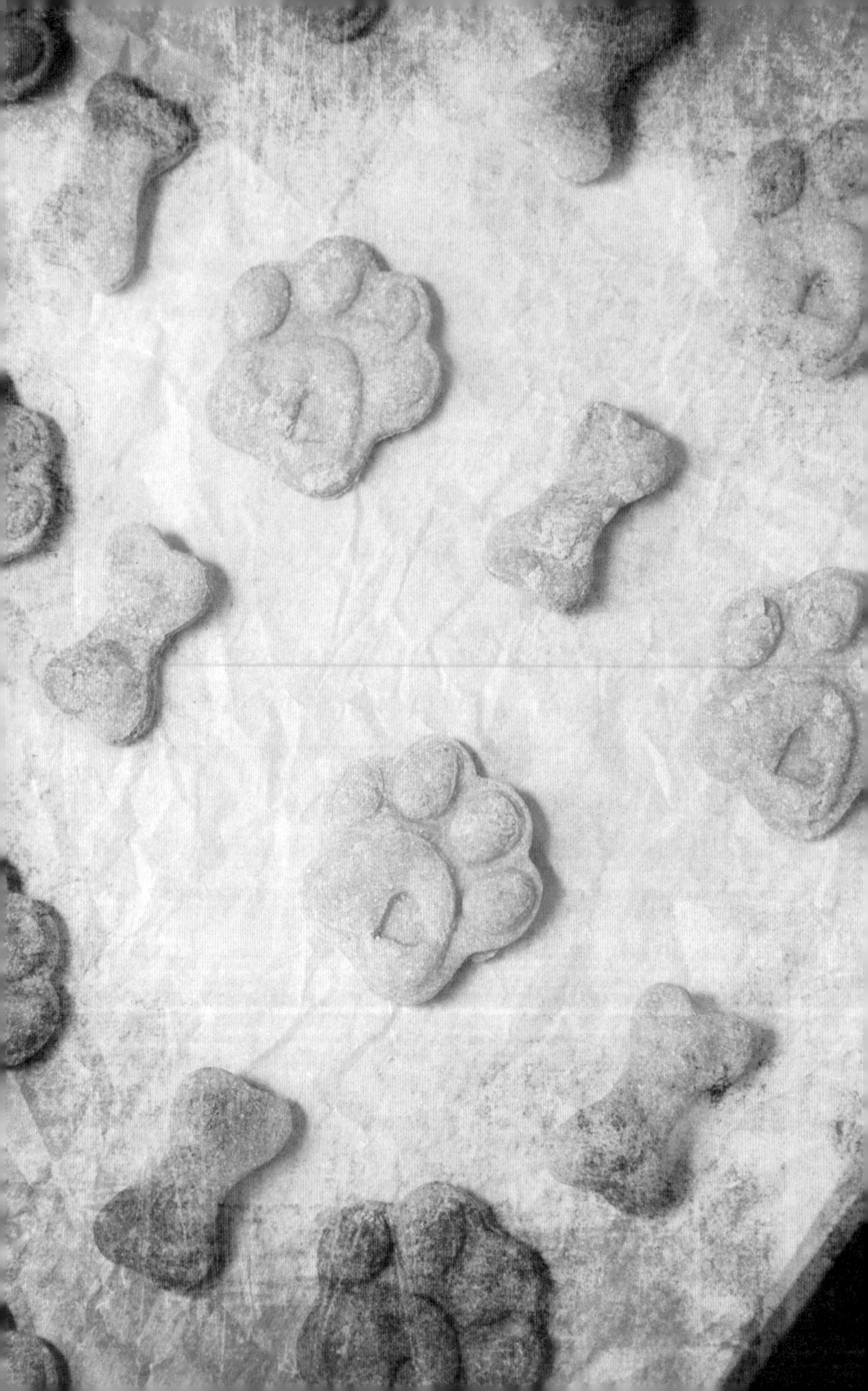

Claws In the Dark

People aren't the only ones who love Main Street in St. Charles—it's also a favorite stop for our four-legged fur babies! Canine Cookies N Cream Dog Bakery at 822 South Main Street makes delicious gourmet dog treats. Turns out, though the living certainly love their canines . . . it seems ghosts do, too!

Molly, the bakery's resident ghost, prefers to come out and play in the winter. Although she is friendly, she makes herself known after hours. The owner will open the shop in the morning to find items have been moved around or things knocked over. Once, a glass jar of dog treats lay broken across the floor.

The bakery's security camera has also captured some interesting events. One evening, a bright light hovered by the cash register and then moved across the room. Before the owner made Canine Cookies her full-time job, she worked at SSM St. Joseph's Hospital in St. Charles, off First Capitol Drive. One of her patient's sons worked on a ghost hunting television show. They swapped creepy stories, and the bakery owner showed him the video of the light. The son confirmed ghost activity happening in her store.

Canine Cookies' neighbor used to be a gift shop at one time. The owners agreed that Molly either didn't like the gift shop or the owner (or maybe both!). One morning, the gift shop's owner unlocked the front door to find her four-foot glass shelf knocked over onto the ground. The shelf hadn't been damaged but every item on it was broken. They believed Molly was delivering a message.

But—how did the owners know the ghost's name was Molly? The gift shop owner often worked late into the night, all alone in the empty store. That's when she'd hear mysterious voices echoing around her. One name kept floating through the air: Molly.

Lewis & Clark Monument, Frontier Park

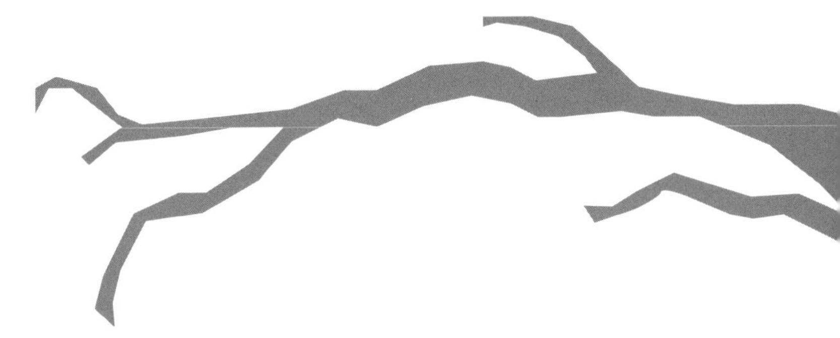

A Ghostly Goodbye

You've survived the stroll down the streets of St. Charles through these spooky stories. Are you ready to visit in person? Bring a friend with you. There's safety in numbers.

You never know when past pioneers and explorers will show up. Two hundred years is an eternity with no one to spook with. Maybe you'll see history come to life and have your own chilling tale to share.

Listen for whispered words, cackling laughter, and rolling marbles. Keep your eyes peeled for phantom children, window watchers, and flickering lights. If you feel a tingling sensation crawl up your spine, remember to trust your instincts. You now know what roams the streets of St. Charles.

Bibliography

Adrian. (2025, April 11). Aquarian Herbs Owner. (N. Jacobsmeyer, Interviewer)

Aerial. (2025, April 7). Grandma's Cookie Employee. (N. Jacobsmeyer, Interviewer)

Bates, C. (2025, April 8). The Main House Owner. (N. Jacobsmeyer, Interviewer)

Berlener, L. (2025, April 11). U Defined Boutique Owner. (N. Jacobsmeyer, Interviewer)

Braddens 1818 Bistrot. (2025). Retrieved April 3, 2025, from https://1818bistrot.com/story

Bureau, C. 2. (Producer), & Cranford, S. (Director). (2006). *Mysteries on Main* [Motion Picture].

Bureau, G. S. (2021, October). *St. Charles Haunted History Trail*. Retrieved from Discover St. Charles: https://www.discoverstcharles.com/events/legends-lanterns/haunted-history-trail/

Bureau, G. S. (2025). *St. Charles History*. Retrieved from Discover St. Charles: https://www.discoverstcharles.com/plan-your-visit/about-the-area/history/

Filardi, N. (2025, April 7). Owner. (N. Jacobsmeyer, Interviewer)

Foster, B. (2025, April 4). Director of Lewis and Clark Boat House & Museum. (N. Jacobsmeyer, Interviewer)

Foster, T. (2025, April 4). Lewis & Clark Boat House & Museum employee. (N. Jacobsmeyer, Interviewer)

Geno, E. (2025, March 6). Missouri State Park/First Missouri State Capital employee. (N. Jacobsmeyer, Interviewer)

History Kept Alive. (1982, March 22). *St. Charles Post*.

Hoffman, S., & Feldewerth, T. (2025, March 6). Flower Peddlar & Holiday House owners. (N. Jacobsmeyer, Interviewer)

Holden, M. a. (2025, April 9). Provenance Soapworks Owners. (N. Jacobsmeyer, Interviewer)

Home of David McNair - St. Charles, MO. (2025). Retrieved from Waymarking: https://www.waymarking.com/waymarks/WM3QX1_Home_of_David_McNair

Huffman, P. (2025, January 16). Lindenwood University Archivist/Reference Librarian, Library Services. (N. Jacobsmeyer, Interviewer)

Jane. (2025, April 11). Vintage She Shed owner . (N. Jacobsmeyer, Interviewer)

Keepen, A. (2025, April 11). Native Traditions Gallery Owner. (N. Jacobsmeyer, Interviewer)

Keevin, M. (2025, April 4). Owner. (N. Jacobsmeyer, Interviewer)

Kienzle, V. B. (2022). *Main Street St. Charles, MO: A Walk Through History*. St. Louis: Reedy Press.

Kirkwood, K. (2025, March 6). Lewis & Clark Restaurant, previous owner. (N. Jacobsmeyer, Interviewer)

La Rose, C. (2025, April 11). 337 by La Roserie Owner. (N. Jacobsmeyer, Interviewer)

McMichael, A. (2025, March 6). Once Upon A Time owner. (N. Jacobsmeyer, Interviewer)

Members, C. (2025). *History of the Parish*. Retrieved from St. Borromeo Church: https://stcharlesborromeo.connectingmembers.com/About/History

Mendoza, D. M. (2018, December 8). *Death and Mourning Practices in the Victorian Age*. Retrieved from Psychology Today: https://www.psychologytoday.com/us/blog/understanding-grief/201812/death-and-mourning-practices-in-the-victorian-age?msockid=2f291ae833aa624429140e5f32c56318

Morschl, K. (2025, February 28). Siostra Polish Pottery. (N. Jacobsmeyer, Interviewer)

Moss, N. (2025, April 11). MOss Boutique Owner. (N. Jacobsmeyer, Interviewer)

Natalie. (2025, April 4). Employee. (N. Jacobsmeyer, Interviewer)

Neighbors, J. (2013, October 11). *Haunted Towns of the Midwest - St Charles, Missouri*. Retrieved from A Grave Interest: https://agraveinterest.blogspot.com/2013/10/haunted-towns-of-midwest-st-charles.html

Offutt, J. (2007). *Haunted Missouri: A Ghostly Guide to the Show-Me State's Most Spirited Spots*. Kirksville: Truman State University Press.

O'Keefe, B. &. (2025, April 8). Mad Hatter Attiques & More Owners. (N. Jacobsmeyer, Interviewer)

Parks, M. S. (n.d.). Launching Pad of Statehood. *First Missouri State Capitol State Historic Site*. St. Charles, Missouri: Missouri Department of Natural Resources.

Payton. (2025, April 7). Grandma's Cookie Employee. (N. Jacobsmeyer, Interviewer)

Powell, V. (n.d.). Historic 1792 St. Charles Borromeo Log Church. St. Charles, Missouri: JQH H.P. for Education.

Resources, M. D. (2014, June). First Missouri State Capitrol State Historic Site. *Missouri State Parks*. St. Charles, Missouri: Missouri Department of Natural Resources.

SCCHS. Castile, R. (2002, October 23). Ghosts Reportedly Protect Historic Buildings. *St. Charles Journal*. Ghost Stories Collection.

SCCHS. Farmers Tavern, 700 South Main Street.

SCCHS. Ghost Watches Over Lindenwood Students. (2007, October 28). *St. Charles Journal*, pp. 81-82. Ghost Stories Collection.

SCCHS. Historic Sites Survey Report Form. 337 South Main Street.

SCCHS. Historic Sites Survey Report Form. 407 South Main Street.

SCCHS. History Kept Alive. (1982, March 22). *St. Charles Post*.

SCCHS. McElhiney, E. O. (1963, April 11). Historical Series - Served As Priest Home. *St. Charles Journal*, p. 1 & 5.

SCCHS. Newbill-McElhiney Home, 625 South Main Street. John Watkins Collection.

SCCHS. Scott, Archie. Personal letter February, 17, 2007. Ghost Stories Collection.

SCCHS. Seaton, R. R. (1992, October 30). Boo! St. Charles County Landmarks Have a History of Hauntings. *St. Peters Star*, pp. 1, 5. Ghost Stories Collection.

SCCHS. Weich, S. (2010, October 31). Lindenwood's Founder is a Ghostly Halloween Legend. *St. Louis Post-Dispatch*, pp. Community, B1. Ghost Stories Collection.

Smith, I. (2016, May 28). *The Rules And Regulations Of Mourning In The Victorian Era*. Retrieved from Vintage News: https://www.thevintagenews.com/2016/05/28/39293-2/

Taylor, T. (2012). *Haunted Missouri: Ghosts and Strange Phenomena of the Show Me State*. Mechanicsburg: Stackpole Books.

University, L. (n.d.). Retrieved from Lindenwood University: www.lindenwood.edu

Waymarking. (2025). Retrieved April 3, 2025, from https://www.waymarking.com/waymarks/wm19DR8_501_S_Main_St_St_Charles_Historic_District_St_Charles_MO

NICKI JACOBSMEYER lives in rural Missouri, where she writes fiction and nonfiction for adults and children. She inspires others to discover and dream through reading and believes books are windows to the world. Visit www.nickijacobsmeyer.com to learn more!

Check out some of the other *Spooky America* titles available now!

Also by Nicki Jacobsmeyer: